Usborne

Multiplying
and Dividing
Activity Book

Darran Stobbart

Illustrated by
Luana Rinaldo

Designed by
Jodie Smith, Tilly Kitching
and Katie Webb

Education consultant: Sheila Ebbutt

What are multiplying and dividing?

Multiplying a number means adding it to itself a number of times.
For example...

$$3 + 3 + 3 + 3 = 12$$ can also be written as... $$3 \times 4 = 12$$

...because you're adding the number 3 together 4 times.

Multiplying is also a good way of counting groups of things.

These 5 beetles each have 6 spots on their backs.
How many spots are there altogether?

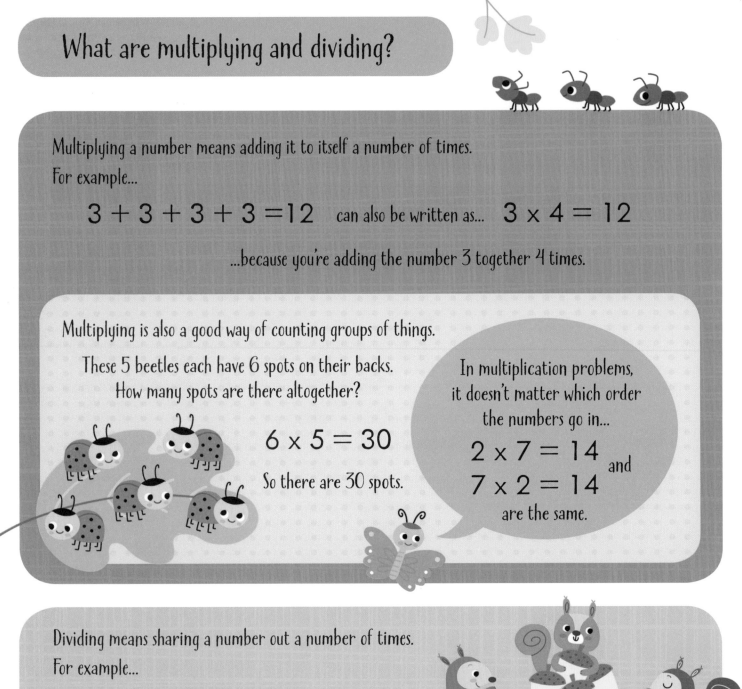

$$6 \times 5 = 30$$

So there are 30 spots.

In multiplication problems, it doesn't matter which order the numbers go in...

$$2 \times 7 = 14$$ and
$$7 \times 2 = 14$$

are the same.

Dividing means sharing a number out a number of times.
For example...

If there are 12 acorns, how many does each squirrel get?

$$12 \div 3 = 4$$

You're sharing 12 between 3, which means each squirrel gets 4.

How to use this book

This book will give you lots of different ways of solving multiplication and division questions. It doesn't matter which you use — just pick the one that works best for you. The book is split into six parts...

Start out multiplying: pages 4 – 13

Discover how to multiply by counting in groups and using grids.

Times tables: pages 14 – 27

Use the times tables to multiply.

Start out dividing: pages 28 – 39

Discover how to divide by sharing things out and using a number line.

Fractions and remainders: pages 40 – 45

What to do when your division answer isn't a whole number.

Doing the opposite: pages 46 – 49

Solve problems using the relationship between multiplying and dividing.

Big numbers: pages 50 – 53

How to multiply and divide big numbers.

Don't worry if you get stuck. Just turn to the answer pages at the back of this book.

Quick quizzes let you check what you've learned so far. Give yourself a star from the sticker pages for each quiz you complete.

Counting in groups

Multiplication is a way of counting things in groups. Instead of counting each thing individually, you multiply the number of things in each group by the number of groups.

For example, how many wings do these 4 birds have?

To work it out, you could count each wing: 1, 2, 3...
You could count up in twos: 2, 4, 6...

Or you could multiply:
2 x 4 = 8

The leaves on these sunflowers grow in pairs. Counting up in twos, work out how many leaves there are altogether on each plant, and write it below.

2 x 3 =   2 x 4 =   2 x 5 =   2 x 10 =

Each pod contains 10 beans. How many beans are there altogether?

Count up in 10s, using this space for any working out.

$10 \times 9 = 90$

These tomato seeds are being planted in rows of 5. How many plants will grow here?

Count up in 5s, using this space for any working out.

$5 \times 6 = 30$

Each potato plant has 3 potatoes growing underground. How many potatoes are there?

Count up in 3s, using this space for any working out.

$3 \times 3 = 9$

Make it bigger

Multiplying is a way of making numbers **bigger**.

Each robot needs 2 jars of motor oil. Using the stickers from the back of the book, place enough jars on the trays for...

Doubling means making something **twice** as big, or **multiplying by 2.**

Tripling means making something **three** times as big, or **multiplying by 3.**

2x as many robots

3x as many robots

6x as many robots

Each one of these robots needs 3 power crystals to run for a day. How many power crystals will they need to run for...

five times longer?

twice as long?

seven times longer?

Use this space for any working out.

Multiplying by 10

Numbers are usually written in columns, as on this robot. The value of each number depends on which column it is in. This is known as place value.

The columns get 10x bigger each time you move left. This makes multiplying by 10 especially easy.

When you multiply a number by 10, it becomes 10 times bigger – so all the numbers move one column to the left, and you add a 0 in the units column.

x 10   x 10

Hundreds	Tens	Units
7	**7**	**7**

For example...

$$7 \times 10 = 70$$

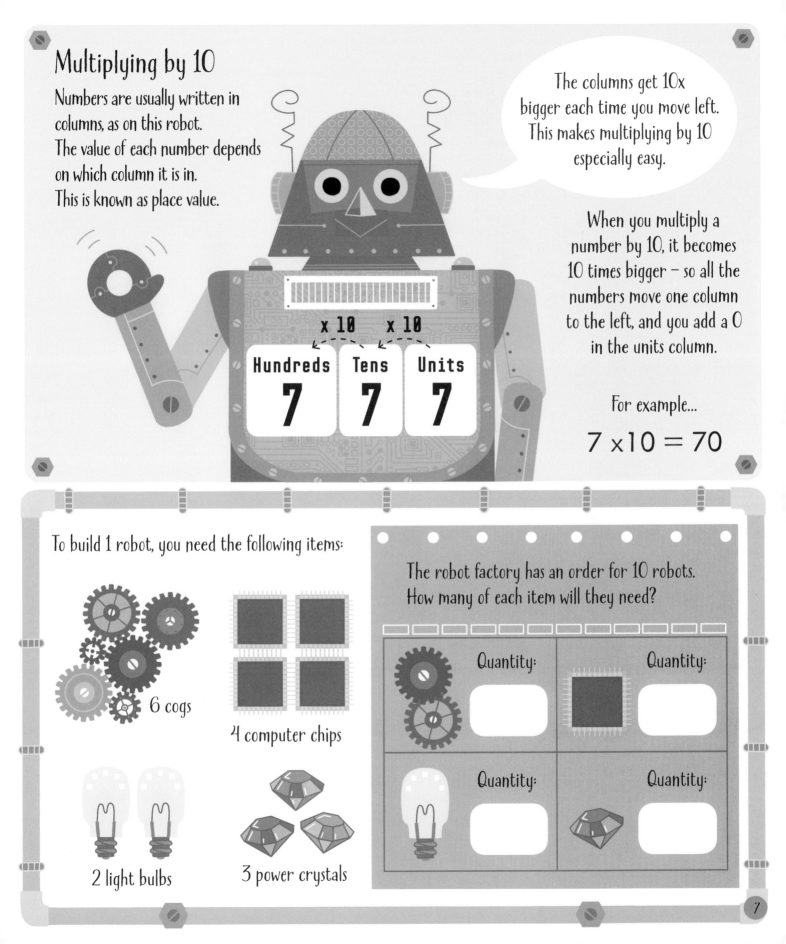

To build 1 robot, you need the following items:

6 cogs

4 computer chips

2 light bulbs

3 power crystals

The robot factory has an order for 10 robots. How many of each item will they need?

Quantity:

Quantity:

Quantity:

Quantity:

Using arrays to multiply

Another way of multiplying is by using a grid known as an **array**.

In this array, there are 6 cupcakes along the top...

...and 3 down the side.

To work out the total number of cupcakes, you multiply the number of rows by the number of columns.

$$3 \times 6 = 18$$

It doesn't matter which way around you write a multiplication.

This tray of brownies has 2 rows of 5.

$$2 \times 5 = 10$$

If you rotate the box this way, it now has five rows of two – but the same total number of brownies.

$$5 \times 2 = 10$$

Can you work out how many cookies there are on each tray?

$3 \times 6 = $ ....

$4 \times 2 = $ ....

$9 \times 2 = $ ....

$4 \times 4 = $ ....

Using stickers from the back of the book, can you create an array of 3 x 5 cookies?

How many cookies is that in total?

$3 \times 5 = $ ....

Arrays can help with bigger numbers, too. This tray has 13 cupcakes along the top, and 3 down the side.

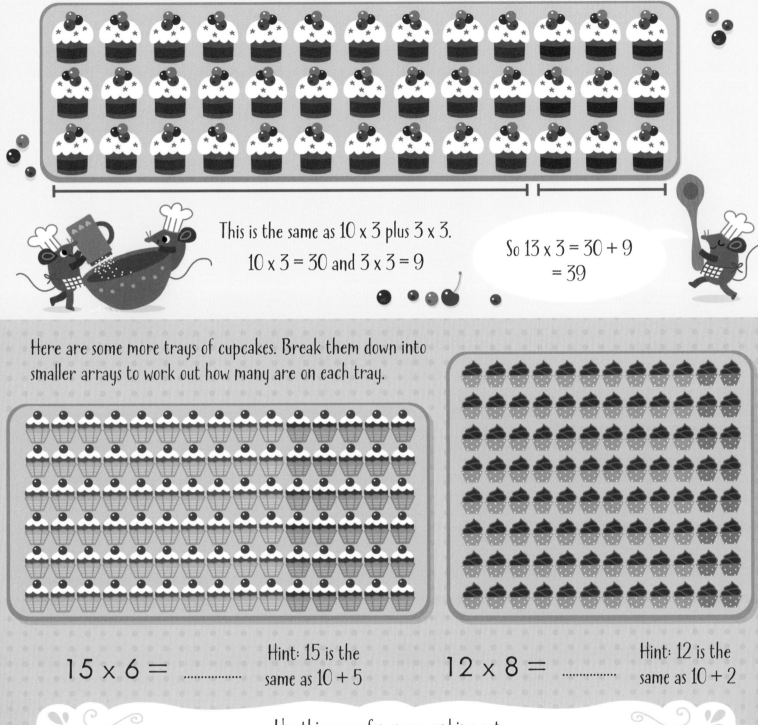

This is the same as 10 x 3 plus 3 x 3.

10 x 3 = 30 and 3 x 3 = 9

So 13 x 3 = 30 + 9
= 39

Here are some more trays of cupcakes. Break them down into smaller arrays to work out how many are on each tray.

15 x 6 = ...

Hint: 15 is the same as 10 + 5

12 x 8 = ...

Hint: 12 is the same as 10 + 2

Use this space for your working out.

Using a number line

One way of multiplying is by counting along a number line.
For example, 6 x 4 means making 4 jumps of 6, like this...

Always
start at 0

+6   +6   +6   +6

0 1 2 3 4 5 6 7 8 9 10 11 12 13 14 15 16 17 18 19 20 21 22 23 24

This penguin is jumping along these rocks in 2s. Can you use the number line to work out where it will be after...

2 jumps of 2   3 jumps of 2   5 jumps of 2

Remember
to start at 0

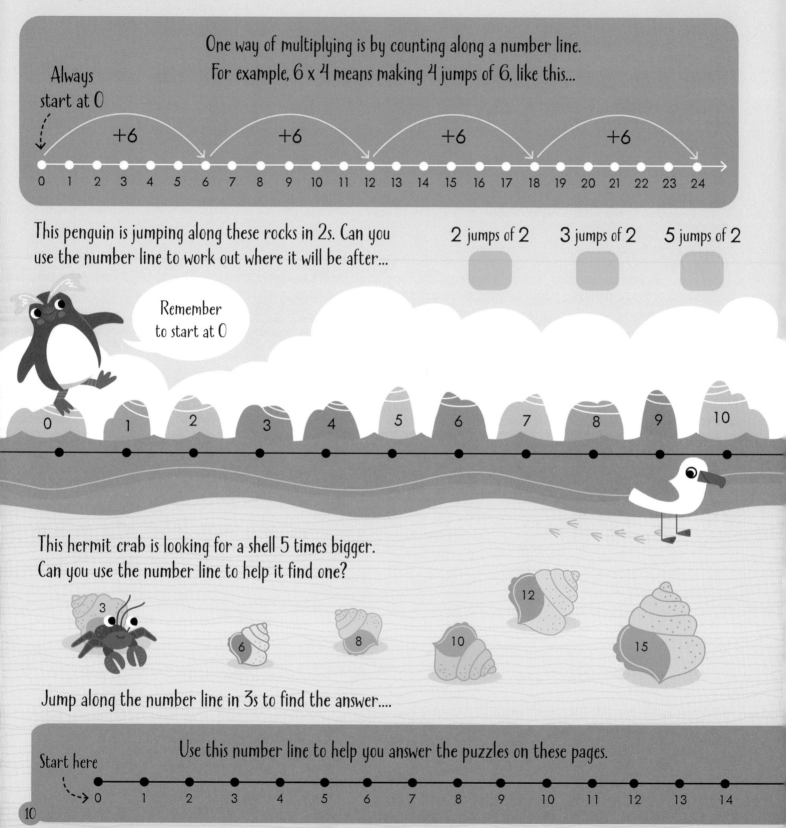

0   1   2   3   4   5   6   7   8   9   10

This hermit crab is looking for a shell 5 times bigger.
Can you use the number line to help it find one?

3

6   8   10   12   15

Jump along the number line in 3s to find the answer....

Use this number line to help you answer the puzzles on these pages.

Start here

0 1 2 3 4 5 6 7 8 9 10 11 12 13 14

This seal is hunting for fish! Can you help it find its way through the seaweed by using the number line to answer the questions?

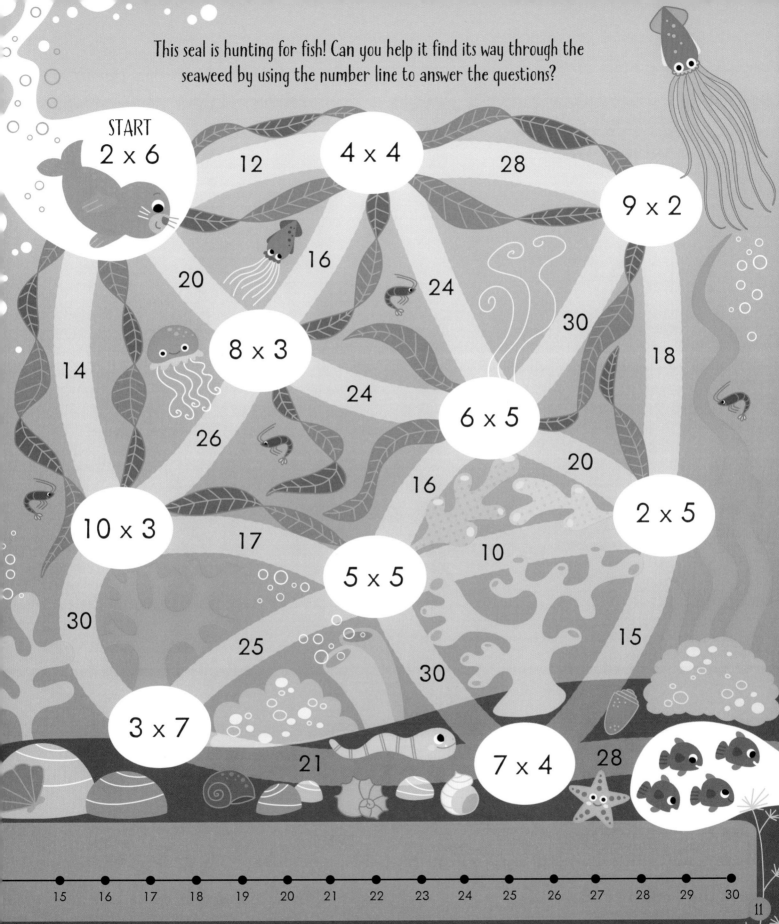

START
2 x 6

12

4 x 4

28

9 x 2

16

20

24

8 x 3

30

18

24

6 x 5

26

16

20

14

10 x 3

17

5 x 5

10

2 x 5

30

25

15

3 x 7

30

21

7 x 4

28

15 16 17 18 19 20 21 22 23 24 25 26 27 28 29 30

Add stickers from the sticker page, so that each dog has 2 bows.

How many bows is that altogether? $2 \times 4 =$ ☐

Dog Salon

Each dog eats 7 dog treats while being groomed. How many get eaten in total?

$7 \times 3 =$ ☐

If it takes one bottle of shampoo to wash 5 puppies, how many can be washed with 3 bottles?

$5 \times 3 =$ ☐

The dog salon goes through this many items each day.
Complete the order form for seven days.

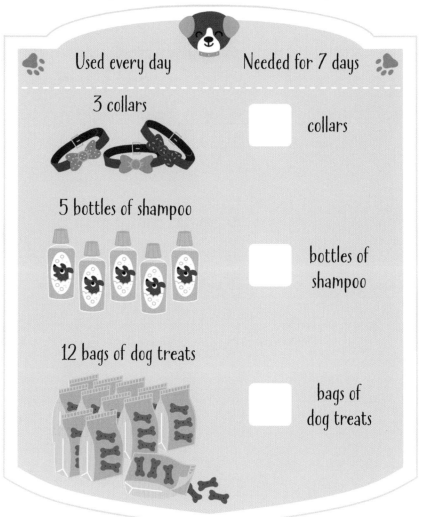

Used every day	Needed for 7 days
3 collars	☐ collars
5 bottles of shampoo	☐ bottles of shampoo
12 bags of dog treats	☐ bags of dog treats

These dogs need to have their claws trimmed. Each dog has 4 paws, and there are 5 claws on each paw. How many claws need trimming in total?

$5 \times 8 =$ ☐ claws

It takes the stylist 10 minutes to trim the fur on one terrier.
How many minutes will it take to trim...

4 terriers ☐ minutes

6 terriers ☐ minutes

7 terriers ☐ minutes

2x, 4x and 8x tables

Times tables are lists of multiplication statements. If you know your tables, you can work out the answers to multiplication questions quickly and easily.

You can also use the tables to answer division questions, because each multiplication statement has a family of related multiplication and division facts.

For example:

$2 \times 7 = 14$

also tells you...

$7 \times 2 = 14$

$14 \div 2 = 7$

$14 \div 7 = 2$

2x	4x	8x
$2 \times 1 = 2$	$4 \times 1 = 4$	$8 \times 1 = 8$
$2 \times 2 = 4$	$4 \times 2 = 8$	$8 \times 2 = 16$
$2 \times 3 = 6$	$4 \times 3 = 12$	$8 \times 3 = 24$
$2 \times 4 = 8$	$4 \times 4 = 16$	$8 \times 4 = 32$
$2 \times 5 = 10$	$4 \times 5 = 20$	$8 \times 5 = 40$
$2 \times 6 = 12$	$4 \times 6 = 24$	$8 \times 6 = 48$
$2 \times 7 = 14$	$4 \times 7 = 28$	$8 \times 7 = 56$
$2 \times 8 = 16$	$4 \times 8 = 32$	$8 \times 8 = 64$
$2 \times 9 = 18$	$4 \times 9 = 36$	$8 \times 9 = 72$
$2 \times 10 = 20$	$4 \times 10 = 40$	$8 \times 10 = 80$
$2 \times 11 = 22$	$4 \times 11 = 44$	$8 \times 11 = 88$
$2 \times 12 = 24$	$4 \times 12 = 48$	$8 \times 12 = 96$

The 2x, 4x and 8x tables go together, because the 4x answers are double the 2x ones, and the 8x answers are double the 4x ones.

Using the tables, can you answer the questions on these two pages?

Each leaf is home to 2 snails. Add the right number of snail stickers from the back of the book, and work out the total for each plant.

A dragonfly has 4 wings. How many wings do 4 dragonflies have in total?

....

If each bee visits 4 flowers, how many flowers will...

3 bees visit?

....

7 bees visit?

....

6 bees visit?

....

These spiders eat 1 fly every 8 days. Using stickers from the sticker pages, add enough flies to each web to keep the spiders fed for...

16 days

24 days

48 days

5x and 10x tables

The 5x and 10x tables go together because the answers in the 5x table are half the answers in the 10x.

> The answers in the 10x table all end in 0.

> If you multiply an **even** number by 5, the answer ends in 0. When you multiply an **odd** number by 5, the answer ends in 5.

5 x	10 x
$5 \times 1 = 5$	$10 \times 1 = 10$
$5 \times 2 = 10$	$10 \times 2 = 20$
$5 \times 3 = 15$	$10 \times 3 = 30$
$5 \times 4 = 20$	$10 \times 4 = 40$
$5 \times 5 = 25$	$10 \times 5 = 50$
$5 \times 6 = 30$	$10 \times 6 = 60$
$5 \times 7 = 35$	$10 \times 7 = 70$
$5 \times 8 = 40$	$10 \times 8 = 80$
$5 \times 9 = 45$	$10 \times 9 = 90$
$5 \times 10 = 50$	$10 \times 10 = 100$
$5 \times 11 = 55$	$10 \times 11 = 110$
$5 \times 12 = 60$	$10 \times 12 = 120$

The hike to the lost temple on the opposite page takes 5 days. Below are some of the supplies the explorers use every day. How much will they need for the hike there – and for the hike there and back again?

3 cans of beans

7 energy bars

5 bananas

Supplies for the hike there:

Energy bars

Bananas

Cans of beans

Supplies for there and back:

Energy bars

Bananas

Cans of beans

Can you help this explorer through the jungle? Answer the questions to find the safe route to the ancient ruin.

START
3 x 5

55

2 x 10

110

15

20

4 x 5

85

9 x 5

45

7 x 10

105

20

50

8 x 5

40

9 x 10

60

90

6 x 10

70

65

7 x 5

75

30

35

5

66

6 x 5

100

FINISH

12 x 10

120

3x, 6x and 9x tables

These tables go together because the 6x answers are double the 3x ones, and the 9x answers are the same as the answers in the 3x and 6x tables added together.

The numbers in the answers to the 6x table always add up to a number in the 3x table.
$6 \times 8 = 48$ and $4 + 8 = 12$

If you add up the numbers of the first ten 9x answers, they always add up to 9. For example,
$9 \times 3 = 27$ and $2 + 7 = 9$

3 x
$3 \times 1 = 3$
$3 \times 2 = 6$
$3 \times 3 = 9$
$3 \times 4 = 12$
$3 \times 5 = 15$
$3 \times 6 = 18$
$3 \times 7 = 21$
$3 \times 8 = 24$
$3 \times 9 = 27$
$3 \times 10 = 30$
$3 \times 11 = 33$
$3 \times 12 = 36$

6 x
$6 \times 1 = 6$
$6 \times 2 = 12$
$6 \times 3 = 18$
$6 \times 4 = 24$
$6 \times 5 = 30$
$6 \times 6 = 36$
$6 \times 7 = 42$
$6 \times 8 = 48$
$6 \times 9 = 54$
$6 \times 10 = 60$
$6 \times 11 = 66$
$6 \times 12 = 72$

9 x
$9 \times 1 = 9$
$9 \times 2 = 18$
$9 \times 3 = 27$
$9 \times 4 = 36$
$9 \times 5 = 45$
$9 \times 6 = 54$
$9 \times 7 = 63$
$9 \times 8 = 72$
$9 \times 9 = 81$
$9 \times 10 = 90$
$9 \times 11 = 99$
$9 \times 12 = 108$

Hit all the numbers in the 3x table to win the top prize! Add stickers from the sticker pages to the ones you need to hit.

TOP PRIZE

Fill in the missing answers below. Then find the matching ducks and shade them in.

6 x 2 = ...   6 x 11 = ...

6 x 5 = ...

6 x 7 = ...   6 x 3 = ...

This Ferris wheel takes 6 minutes to make one full turn. How many turns could it make in...

12 minutes?   30 minutes?   42 minutes?

What do you get if you multiply the numbers on each pair of bumper cars together? Add the right sticker in the crashes.

7x, 11x and 12x tables

The 7x, 11x and 12x tables don't fit into groups.

If it feels like a lot to learn, just remember that you've seen most of them in the other times tables already.

Tip: To remember $7 \times 8 = 56$, write it backwards: $56 = 7 \times 8$

5, 6, 7, 8

Can you see the pattern in the 11x table, up to 11×9?

7 x

7×1	$= 7$
7×2	$= 14$
7×3	$= 21$
7×4	$= 28$
7×5	$= 35$
7×6	$= 42$
7×7	$= 49$
7×8	$= 56$
7×9	$= 63$
7×10	$= 70$
7×11	$= 77$
7×12	$= 84$

11 x

11×1	$= 11$
11×2	$= 22$
11×3	$= 33$
11×4	$= 44$
11×5	$= 55$
11×6	$= 66$
11×7	$= 77$
11×8	$= 88$
11×9	$= 99$
11×10	$= 110$
11×11	$= 121$
11×12	$= 132$

12 x

12×1	$= 12$
12×2	$= 24$
12×3	$= 36$
12×4	$= 48$
12×5	$= 60$
12×6	$= 72$
12×7	$= 84$
12×8	$= 96$
12×9	$= 108$
12×10	$= 120$
12×11	$= 132$
12×12	$= 144$

This rocket takes 7 days to get from one planet to the next. How long will it take to reach...

Start!

Planet 1

....

Planet 2

....

Planet 3

....

The panels on these rockets need eleven screws each. How many screws will it take to repair each rocket? Add stickers from the sticker pages to complete each rocket.

5 panels missing

3 panels missing

Each planet takes a different number of days to go around this sun. Can you use the clues to fill in the gaps?

Klip

.... days

Klip takes 5 days to go around once. How long does it take to go around 7 times?

Jenks

.... days

Jenks takes 12 days to go around once. How long will it take to go around 9 times?

Grum

.... days

Grum takes 7 days to go around once. How long will it take to go around 8 times?

Ensk

.... days

Ensk takes 11 days to go around once. How long will it take to go around 6 times?

Who is winning this game of moonball? Each goal is worth 12 points. The purple team has scored 7 goals, and the blue team has scored 4.

How many points does each team have?

Scoreboard

Purple team

[   ] points

Blue team

[   ] points

21

Number grids

If you shade the answers to the times tables on a number grid, patterns start to appear.

				77	78	79	80	
81	82	83	84	85	86	87	88	89	90
91	92	93	94	95	96	97	98	99	100

2x

1	2	3	4	5	6	7	8	9	10
11	12	13	14	15	16	17	18	19	20
21	22	23	24	25	26	27	28	29	30
31	32	33	34	35	36	37	38	39	40
41	42	43	44	45	46	47	48	49	50
51	52	53	54	55	56	57	58	59	60
61	62	63	64	65	66	67	68	69	70
71	72	73	74	75	76	77	78	79	80
81	82	83	84	85	86	87	88	89	90
91	92	93	94	95	96	97	98	99	100

You can use the pattern to work out the times tables answers.

On this number grid, the 2x table is shaded up to 2 x 12. Continue the pattern to work out the other answers, all the way up to 2 x 50.

5 [ ]

44
66
50
23

90
86
82
32

21   63

Can you continue the patterns to the 3x and 4x table?
The first two rows have been done for you.

3x

1	2	3	4	5	6	7	8	9	10
11	12	13	14	15	16	17	18	19	20
21	22	23	24	25	26	27	28	29	30
31	32	33	34	35	36	37	38	39	40
41	42	43	44	45	46	47	48	49	50
51	52	53	54	55	56	57	58	59	60
61	62	63	64	65	66	67	68	69	70
71	72	73	74	75	76	77	78	79	80
81	82	83	84	85	86	87	88	89	90
91	92	93	94	95	96	97	98	99	100

4x

1	2	3	4	5	6	7	8	9	10
11	12	13	14	15	16	17	18	19	20
21	22	23	24	25	26	27	28	29	30
31	32	33	34	35	36	37	38	39	40
41	42	43	44	45	46	47	48	49	50
51	52	53	54	55	56	57	58	59	60
61	62	63	64	65	66	67	68	69	70
71	72	73	74	75	76	77	78	79	80
81	82	83	84	85	86	87	88	89	90
91	92	93	94	95	96	97	98	99	100

15   88
37
91   1   95   3   51

5x

1	2	3	4	5	6	7	8	9	10
11	12	13	14	15	16	17	18	19	20
21	22	23	24	25	26	27	28	29	30
31	32	33	34	35	36	37	38	39	40
41	42	43	44	45	46	47	48	49	50
51	52	53	54	55	56	57	58	59	60
61	62	63	64	65	66	67	68	69	70
71	72	73	74	75	76	77	78	79	80
81	82	83	84	85	86	87	88	89	90
91	92	93	94	95	96	97	98	99	100

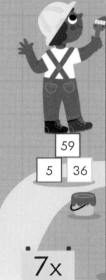

59

5   36

6x

1	2	3	4	5	6	7	8	9	10
11	12	13	14	15	16	17	18	19	20
21	22	23	24	25	26	27	28	29	30
31	32	33	34	35	36	37	38	39	40
41	42	43	44	45	46	47	48	49	50
51	52	53	54	55	56	57	58	59	60
61	62	63	64	65	66	67	68	69	70
71	72	73	74	75	76	77	78	79	80
81	82	83	84	85	86	87	88	89	90
91	92	93	94	95	96	97	98	99	100

7x

1	2	3	4	5	6	7	8	9	10
11	12	13	14	15	16	17	18	19	20
21	22	23	24	25	26	27	28	29	30
31	32	33	34	35	36	37	38	39	40
41	42	43	44	45	46	47	48	49	50
51	52	53	54	55	56	57	58	59	60
61	62	63	64	65	66	67	68	69	70
71	72	73	74	75	76	77	78	79	80
81	82	83	84	85	86	87	88	89	90
91	92	93	94	95	96	97	98	99	100

If you can't see the pattern right away, just keep counting on in 7s.

9x

1	2	3	4	5	6	7	8	9	10
11	12	13	14	15	16	17	18	19	20
21	22	23	24	25	26	27	28	29	30
31	32	33	34	35	36	37	38	39	40
41	42	43	44	45	46	47	48	49	50
51	52	53	54	55	56	57	58	59	60
61	62	63	64	65	66	67	68	69	70
71	72	73	74	75	76	77	78	79	80
81	82	83	84	85	86	87	88	89	90
91	92	93	94	95	96	97	98	99	100

8x

1	2	3	4	5	6	7	8	9	10
11	12	13	14	15	16	17	18	19	20
21	22	23	24	25	26	27	28	29	30
31	32	33	34	35	36	37	38	39	40
41	42	43	44	45	46	47	48	49	50
51	52	53	54	55	56	57	58	59	60
61	62	63	64	65	66	67	68	69	70
71	72	73	74	75	76	77	78	79	80
81	82	83	84	85	86	87	88	89	90
91	92	93	94	95	96	97	98	99	100

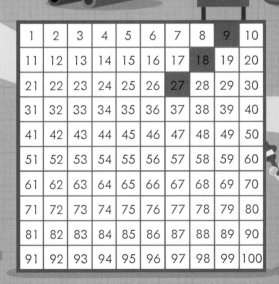

10
20
30

How many of each type of
seed are there in total below?

Pea: 4 seeds per pack

....
pea seeds

Tomato: 10 seeds per pack

....
tomato
seeds

Pumpkin: 6 seeds per pack

....
pumpkin
seeds

If there are 5 garden gnomes on each shelf,
how many gnomes are in stock?

$5 \times 3 =$ [ ] gnomes

If one tub of plant food will feed 4 plants,
how many plants can be fed with 9 tubs?

$9 \times 4 =$ [ ]

Connect the dots
in the 7x table
to find out what
kind of plant is
being sold here.

25 •
42 •
54 •
35 •   49 •
66 •
21
37 •   63 •   • 70
14 •
28 •   56 •   77 •
7
84 •   81 •

24

The leaves on this vine grow in 2s. Add 3 more sets of leaves, using stickers from the sticker pages.

How many leaves does the vine have now?

.... leaves

One hanging basket can take 4 plants in it. How many plants can be grown in...

3 baskets?   9 baskets?   12 baskets?

☐   ☐   ☐

Each head on these flytrap plants catches 3 flies. How many will each plant catch altogether?

☐ flies   ☐ flies   ☐ flies

Find the answers to the multiplications below.

9 groups of 6 seeds

$6 \times 9 =$

5 beetles with 7 spots

$7 \times 5 =$

4 flowers with 4 petals

$4 \times 4 =$

3 constellations with 7 stars

$3 \times 7 =$

Score

Sticker

4

How many will you have?

5x as many fish

$5 \times 4 =$

6x as many coins

$6 \times 5 =$

twice as many seagulls

$2 \times 3 =$

10x as many jewels

$10 \times 9 =$

8x as many crabs

$8 \times 2 =$

Score

Sticker

5

How many blocks are in each array?

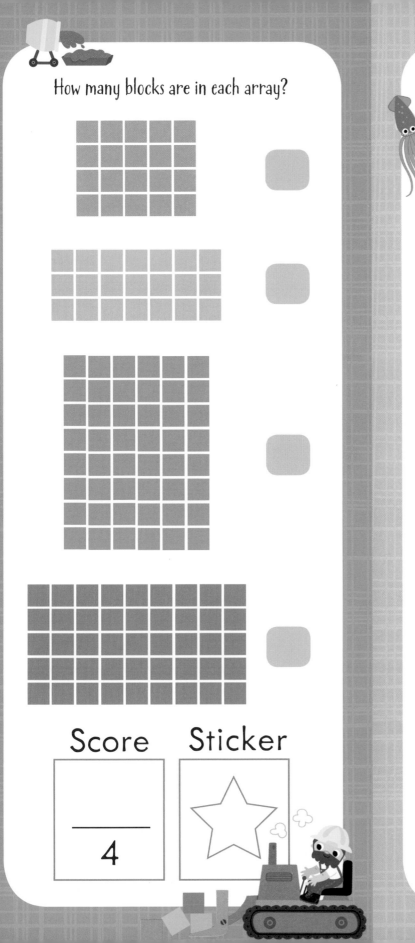

Complete the multiplication statements.

2 x 5 =

6 x ☐ = 54

☐ x 4 = 48

7 x ☐ = 21

8 x 6 =

9 x ☐ = 18

☐ x 8 = 56

10 x 10 =

3 x ☐ = 18

Score

Sticker

4

Score

Sticker

9

27

Sharing it out

Dividing is a way of sharing things equally.
For example...

5 pirates are sharing their loot.
If they have 20 gold coins to divide equally,
how many do they get each?

If each pirate takes one coin, that makes 5 coins.
How many groups of 5 coins can they make?

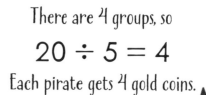

There are 4 groups, so

$$20 \div 5 = 4$$

Each pirate gets 4 gold coins.

Divide the jewels into groups of 5, and count the number of groups.

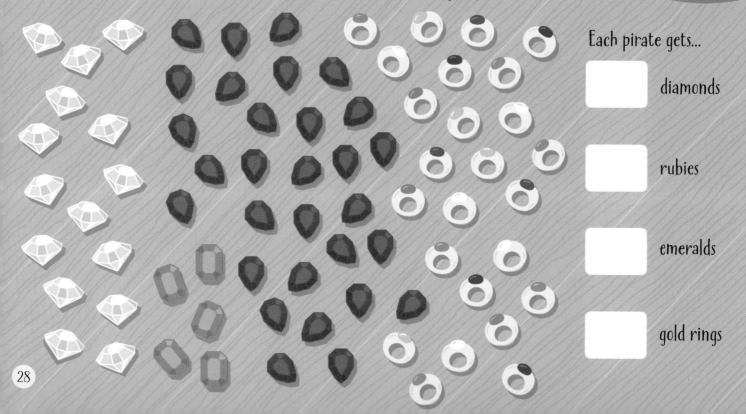

Each pirate gets...

	diamonds
	rubies
	emeralds
	gold rings

Sometimes when you're dividing, you end up with a bit left over – known as a remainder (r).

For example...

There are 7 treasure chests and 2 boats, which can carry 3 chests each. What happens if you try to share the chests equally between the boats?

$$7 \div 2 = 3 \ r1$$
The 'r' means remainder.

This ship has 14 cannonballs and 6 cannons. If each cannon fires the same number, how many cannonballs will be left over?

$$14 \div 6 = \boxed{} \ r \ \boxed{}$$

6 pirates are having a meal. They have 9 fish to share equally, how many whole fish does each pirate get – and how many are left over?

$$9 \div 6 = \boxed{} \ r \ \boxed{}$$

They also have 13 sea biscuits. If they're shared equally, how many are left?

$$13 \div 6 = \boxed{} \ r \ \boxed{}$$

Take it away

Another way of dividing is by **taking away**.

For example, to work out...

$$8 \div 4$$

you count how many times you can take 4 away from 8 until you have nothing left.

$$8 - 4 = 4$$
$$4 - 4 = 0$$

This means you can subtract 4 from 8 twice, so...

$$8 \div 4 = 2$$

This bear has caught 16 fish. If it can swallow 4 in a mouthful, how many mouthfuls will it take to finish them all?

....

Tip: cross out the fish four at a time to help you find the answer.

These 7 marmots have collected 42 leaves in their burrow. If they share them equally, how many leaves will they each get?

$$42 \div 7 =$$

30

There are 15 bags and 5 ponies.
To share the load equally, how many bags should each pony carry?

Tip: cross out the bags five
at a time to get the answer.

$15 \div 5 =$ ☐

There are 36 berries on these bushes and
6 goats. If each goat eats the same number,
how many berries will each goat get?

$36 \div 6 =$ ☐

Making things smaller

Dividing is a way of making numbers **smaller**.

It costs 20 monster pennies for 10 spiders.

This monster only wants **half** that many spiders. How much will that cost?

(Halving means dividing by 2.)

$20 \div 2 =$ ⬤ pennies

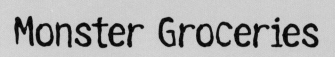

Monster Groceries

10 spiders for 20 pennies

Each of these monsters is buying 20 cans of fizzy slime for their dinner parties tonight. How many cans will each monster get?

It'll just be 2 of us tonight.

There will be 5 of us at dinner this evening.

There'll be 10 of us at dinner.

$20 \div 5 =$ ⬤ $20 \div 10 =$ ⬤ $20 \div 2 =$ ⬤

This monster is shopping for ingredients for stew. The recipe is for 4, but this monster is only cooking for 2. Add the right number of ingredients to the basket using stickers from the sticker pages.

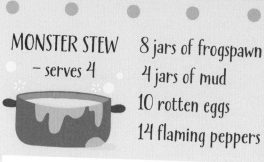

MONSTER STEW
– serves 4

8 jars of frogspawn
4 jars of mud
10 rotten eggs
14 flaming peppers

Use this space for any working out.

5 monsters are buying snacks for a picnic. If they share them equally, how many of each snack will each monster get?

Slime rolls: 10

.... each

Jellied worms: 25

.... each

Earwax flakes: 30

.... each

Toenail bites: 15

.... each

Mud shakes: 5

.... each

Using a number line

You can use a number line to answer division questions.

For example, to work out $16 \div 4$ you start at 16 and count backwards...

Start here.

-4   -4   -4   -4

0 1 2 3 4 5 6 7 8 9 10 11 12 13 14 15 16

It takes 4 jumps, so $16 \div 4 = 4$

Use the number line at the bottom to answer the questions on these pages.

There are 12 ants carrying leaves back to their nest. If it takes 3 ants to carry a leaf, how many leaves can they carry altogether?

Start at 12 and jump back in 3s...

Find the answer, then add the right number of leaves from the sticker pages.

$12 \div 3 = \boxed{}$

0 1 2 3 4 5 6 7 8 9 10 11 12 13 14

This branch has 30 berries. If the parrot eats 6 berries a day, how many days until all the berries are gone?

$$30 \div 6 = \boxed{}$$

2 tree frogs catch 10 flies. If each frog gets the same number, how many is that?

Buzzzzzz

Buzzzzzz

Buzzzzzz

$$10 \div 2 = \boxed{}$$

15 16 17 18 19 20 21 22 23 24 25 26 27 28 29 30

BEACH SHOP

There are 12 buckets to display on these shelves.

Add stickers from the sticker pages so that each shelf has the same number.

$12 \div 3 =$ ⬜

All these beach balls are missing the same number. Can you work out what it is and fill it in?

$36 \div$ ⬜ $= 12$

$12 \div$ ⬜ $= 4$

$9 \div$ ⬜ $= 3$

Can you finish the designs on these surfboards
by shading them using the key below?

KEY

Orange = $42 \div 6$
Yellow = $32 \div 8$
Pink = $110 \div 11$
Blue = $24 \div 2$
Purple = $90 \div 10$
Green = $35 \div 7$

We've collected 21 shells.

If we share them out equally, how many shells do we get each?

$21 \div 3 = \boxed{}$

Halve the ingredients
on this recipe.

10 toenail flakes

14 rotten eggs

4 jars of mud

20 slime rolls

18 flaming peppers

Score   Sticker

_____
5

How many times can you take away...

6 from 18 ?

3 from 21 ?

5 from 30 ?

Share the flies equally between the spiders.

16 flies and 4 spiders

10 flies and 5 spiders

Score   Sticker

_____
5

Find the answers to these division questions.

$30 \div 5 =$

$24 \div 8 =$

$63 \div 7 =$

$144 \div 12 =$

$12 \div 4 =$

$90 \div 9 =$

$48 \div 12 =$

$55 \div 11 =$

Score

Sticker

$\dfrac{\quad}{8}$

Fill in the missing numbers.

$\square \div 10 = 10$

$20 \div \square = 10$

$\square \div 6 = 6$

$40 \div \square = 5$

$\square \div 3 = 6$

$8 \div \square = 2$

$\square \div 11 = 9$

$96 \div \square = 8$

Score

Sticker

$\dfrac{\quad}{8}$

Splitting the remainder

If you divide a number by a bigger number, you end up with a **fraction**, or a part of a whole.

For example, if three friends are sharing a chocolate cake, it needs to be divided into fractions...

Each person gets one third, written like this...

$$\frac{1}{3}$$

← - - - This is the amount you started with.

← - - - This is the number you're dividing by.

Can you match these picnic foods to the fraction they need to be split into?

1 baguette shared by 2 people.

$\frac{3}{4}$

2 pastries shared by 3 people.

$\frac{1}{2}$

3 cookies shared by 4 people.

$\frac{2}{3}$

This pizza is being divided equally between 4 people.

What fraction of the whole pizza does each person get?

_____

Sometimes when dividing, you want an **exact** answer, without any remainder.
So if you do get a remainder you divide it as well, creating a fraction.

For example, if 13 strawberries are shared between 2 people...

$$13 \div 2 = 6 \text{ r } 1$$

Splitting the remainder gives the exact answer:

$$6 \frac{1}{2} \text{ strawberries each.}$$

Can you help share out the rest of the picnic?
Divide the fruit equally between 4 bowls —
how much fruit goes in each bowl?

Pears

Oranges

Plums

$$5 \div 4 = \boxed{\quad} —$$

$$15 \div 4 = \boxed{\quad} —$$

$$9 \div 4 = \boxed{\quad} —$$

41

Each fairy costume needs 2 wings.
If there are 9 wings, how many costumes can be finished?
Add stickers from the sticker page to complete them.

$9 \div 2 = \boxed{} \text{ r } \boxed{}$

There are 19 buttons, and each pirate coat needs 4 buttons.
How many coats can you finish – and how many buttons will be left over?

Tip: try circling the buttons in 4s to help you find the answer.

$19 \div 4 = \boxed{} \text{ r } \boxed{}$

There are 23 bells and 7 jester hats.
How many bells can go on each hat,
if every hat has to have the same amount?

$23 \div 7 = \boxed{} \, r \, \boxed{}$

Each dinosaur costume needs 9 spikes.
How many costumes can be
completed with 39 spikes?

$39 \div 9 = \boxed{} \; r \; \boxed{}$

3 wands need decorating with the same amount
of sequins. If there are 10 bags of sequins,
how many *whole* bags can be used on each?

$10 \div 3 = \boxed{} \, r \, \boxed{}$

What fraction will
the remainder need
to be split into?

$\dfrac{\boxed{}}{\boxed{}}$

How many will be
left over?

17 coins between 4 pirates [ ] r [ ]

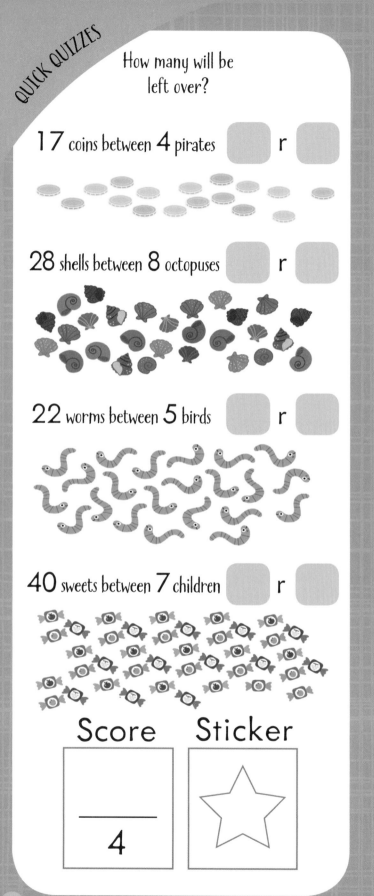

28 shells between 8 octopuses [ ] r [ ]

22 worms between 5 birds [ ] r [ ]

40 sweets between 7 children [ ] r [ ]

Score

Sticker

_____
4

Can you work out
the remainders?

$19 \div 2 = 9$ r [ ]

$23 \div 3 = 7$ r [ ]

$63 \div 10 = 6$ r [ ]

$51 \div 4 = 12$ r [ ]

$27 \div 5 =$ [ ] r [ ]

$58 \div 7 =$ [ ] r [ ]

$33 \div 10 =$ [ ] r [ ]

$29 \div 6 =$ [ ] r [ ]

Score

Sticker

_____
8

What fractions do these need to be divided into for everyone to have an equal share?

1 pizza between 5

―

2 cakes between 3

―

1 apple between 2

―

3 cookies between 4

―

Score

―
4

Sticker

Work out the exact answers to these divisions, showing the remainders as fractions.

$23 \div 2 =$ ☐ ―

$37 \div 3 =$ ☐ ―

$19 \div 4 =$ ☐ ―

$13 \div 2 =$ ☐ ―

$23 \div 3 =$ ☐ ―

$35 \div 4 =$ ☐ ―

Score

―
6

Sticker

45

Back and forth

Because dividing is the opposite of multiplying, if you know the answer to a multiplication question, you can use that to work out the matching division question.

For example, if you know... $5 \times 6 = 30$

then you also know... $30 \div 5 = 6$

and

$30 \div 6 = 5$

This can be shown as a pyramid, like this...

30

÷   ÷

5   ×   6

If you divide the top number by one of the bottom numbers, the answer is the number in the remaining corner.

If you multiply the bottom two numbers, the answer is the number at the top.

Can you fill in the missing numbers on these pyramids?

70

÷   ÷

[   ]   ×   10

[   ]

÷   ÷

3   ×   4

18

÷   ÷

[   ]   ×   2

This wall has some patches missing. Can you fill in the gaps with the correct numbers?

$15 \div 3 =$

$\times 3 = 15$

$16 \div 4 =$

$\times 4 = 16$

$24 \div 6 =$

$\times 6 = 24$

Can you work out the numbers that have been replaced by these symbols?

$14 \div \text{🦎} = 2$
$3 \times \text{🦎} = 21$
$28 \div \text{🦎} = 4$

$\text{🦎} =$

$10 \div \text{⛺} = 2$
$15 \div \text{⛺} = 3$
$4 \times \text{⛺} = 20$

$\text{⛺} =$

Only the bridge with two related statements is safe to cross. Which one is it?

$55 \div 11$

$=$

11×4

$=$

$42 \div 7$

$=$

8×7

$=$

$18 \div 3$

$=$

6×3

$=$

Beware CROCODILES!

47

The package in this party game has a prize every third layer.
If there are 27 layers, how many prizes is that?

$27 \div 3 = \boxed{}$

These cupcakes need decorating. There are 18 chocolate stars on the sticker pages. Can you divide them equally between the cupcakes?

$18 \div 6 = \bigcirc$

There are 7 party bags.
How many treats should go in each?

28 stickers?

14 candies?

7 bouncy balls?

Shade these party balloons using the key.

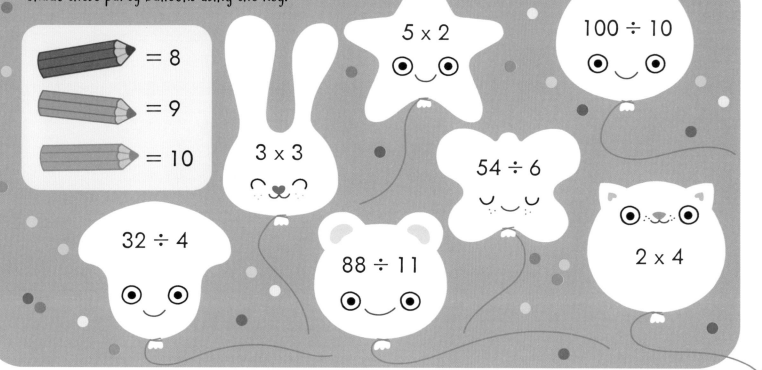

Can you work out which party guest pinned the tail on the donkey?
Pin a ribbon from the sticker page onto the winner.

My tail had the number you get when dividing 12 by 3.

The number on my tail was the answer to 6 x 3.

My tail had the number you divide by 2 to get 10.

The number on mine was the answer to 5 x 5.

Bigger numbers

Multiplying bigger numbers can look tricky, but it's much easier if you work them out in stages.

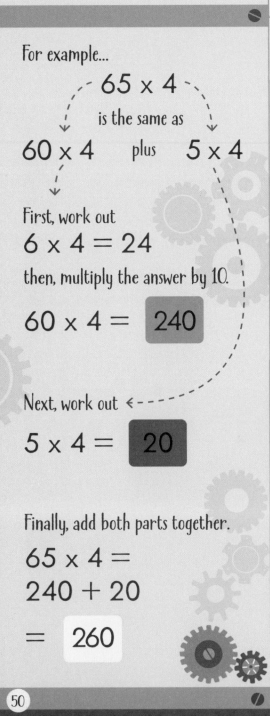

For example...

65×4

is the same as

60×4 plus 5×4

First, work out

$6 \times 4 = 24$

then, multiply the answer by 10.

$60 \times 4 = \boxed{240}$

Next, work out

$5 \times 4 = \boxed{20}$

Finally, add both parts together.

$65 \times 4 =$
$240 + 20$

$= \boxed{260}$

These multiplication problems have been broken down, but some of the parts are missing. Can you work out what they are, and add stickers to fill them in?

28×2

$20 \quad \times \quad \bigcirc \qquad \bigcirc \quad \times \quad 2$

$40 \quad + \quad \bigcirc$

$= \quad \bigcirc$

42×3

$\bigcirc \quad \times \quad 3 \qquad 2 \quad \times \quad \bigcirc$

$\bigcirc \quad + \quad \bigcirc$

$= \quad 126$

These clockwork beetles need finishing.

Can you use the clues to give each the correct shade?

Use this space for your working out.

56 x 3

135

168

304

76 x 4

27 x 5

Work out how many parts will be needed to complete these orders.

ORDER FOR: 5 FLYING HATS

ORDER FOR: 3 CLOCKS

Each flying hat takes 25 screws.

Each clock needs 47 cogs.

25 x 5 = ___ screws

47 x 3 = ___ cogs

Complete the statements – then see if you can match them to their related statements.

15 ÷ 3 = ☐

40 ÷ 5 = ☐

70 ÷ 7 = ☐

96 ÷ 12 = ☐

60 ÷ 5 = ☐

42 ÷ 6 = ☐

36 ÷ 9 = ☐

8 x 5 = ☐

5 x 3 = ☐

9 x 4 = ☐

5 x 12 = ☐

6 x 7 = ☐

12 x 8 = ☐

10 x 7 = ☐

Score   Sticker

$\dfrac{}{7}$

Score   Sticker

$\dfrac{}{7}$

Fill in the gaps in these multiplications to find the final answers.

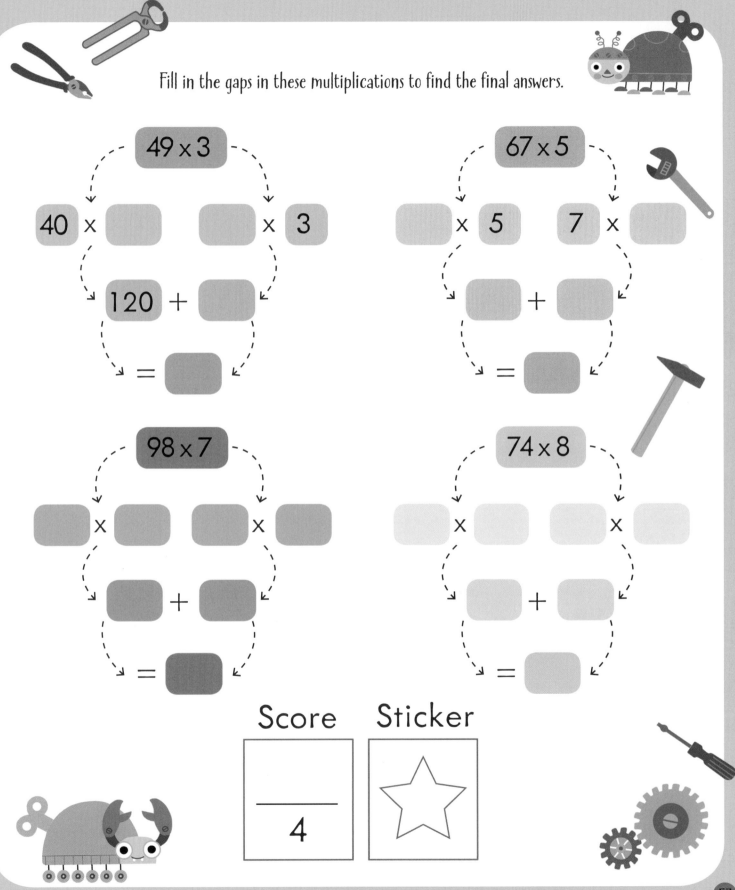

49 × 3

40 × ☐   ☐ × 3

120 + ☐

= ☐

67 × 5

☐ × 5   7 × ☐

☐ + ☐

= ☐

98 × 7

☐ × ☐   ☐ × ☐

☐ + ☐

= ☐

74 × 8

☐ × ☐   ☐ × ☐

☐ + ☐

= ☐

Score

‾4

Sticker

How many windows are there on each of these towers? Write your answers in the shields under each tower.

What a lovely array!

$4 \times 3 =$

$7 \times 4 =$

$6 \times 6 =$

Multiply the numbers on each target by the number in the middle, and write the answers around the edge. The first few have been done for you.

Add an arrow sticker to the biggest answer on each target.

6
9   3 x3 8
12
36

4
11 x6 7
2

7
9   x7 5
10

This knight is on a quest to find a lost crown.
Help him through the maze by solving the clues.

START

How many legs would 7 horses have altogether?

30

The number of letters in

dragon
x5

20

18   28

A baby dragon has 9 spikes on its back. How many spikes will there be when all the dragon's eggs hatch?

12

If this shield has 6 stars, how many stars will 2 shields have?

60

If 10 archers fire 6 arrows each, how many arrows do they use altogether?

71   16

63

26

66

The number of red banners multiplied by the number of blue banners...

There are 7 gold coins in each chest, how many coins are there altogether?

10

If each castle has 8 windows, how many windows are on 10 castles?

80

12

21

18

FINISH

A B C

56

18

I have 9 stems with 6 berries on each. How many berries do I have altogether?

The apple tree outside drops 8 apples a day. How many will it drop in 7 days?

49

What is 49 ÷ 7?

7

88

54

11

4

6

There are 8 rabbit babies in each nest. How many are there altogether?

This rabbit can dig 3 tunnels a day. How many days would it take to dig 12 tunnels?

16

2

I've been collecting shiny stones! I've found 2 a day for the last 10 days. How many is that?

28

What is 24 ÷ 12?

18

20

57

Answers

4–5 Counting in groups

From left to right, the sunflowers have 6, 8, 10 and 20 leaves.

10×9 pods $= 90$ beans in total

$5 \times 6 = 30$ seeds in total

There are 3 groups of 3 potatoes, so altogether there are 9 potatoes.

6–7 Make it bigger

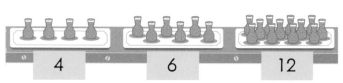

From left to right, the robots need 15 crystals, 6 crystals and 21 crystals.

The robot factory will need to order: 60 cogs, 40 computer chips, 20 light bulbs, 30 power crystals.

8–9 Using arrays to multiply

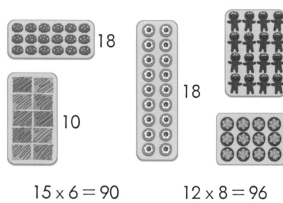

$15 \times 6 = 90$ $12 \times 8 = 96$

10–11 Using a number line

After 2 jumps the penguin will be on number 4.
After 3 jumps, it will be on number 6.
After 5 jumps, it will be on number 10.

The hermit crab needs the shell marked 15.

12–13 More practice

There are 8 bows in total.

The dogs will eat 21 treats altogether.

15 puppies can be washed.

For 7 days, the salon will need: 21 collars, 35 bottles of shampoo and 84 boxes of dog treats.

There are 40 claws on the dogs.

4 terriers will take 40 minutes to trim.
6 terriers will take 60 minutes to trim.
7 terriers will take 70 minutes to trim.

14–15 2x, 4x and 8x tables

The first plant supports 6 snails.
The second plant supports 8 snails.
The third plant supports 10 snails.

4 dragonflies have 16 wings between them.

3 bees will visit 12 flowers.
7 bees will visit 28 flowers.
6 bees will visit 24 flowers.

16–17 5x and 10x tables

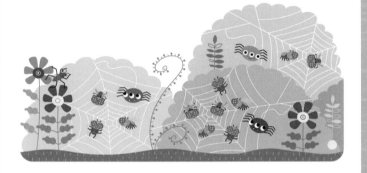

Supplies for the hike there:		Supplies for there and back:	
35	Energy bars	70	Energy bars
25	Bananas	50	Bananas
15	Cans of beans	30	Cans of beans

18–19 3x, 6x and 9x tables

The ducks numbered 12, 66, 30, 42 and 18 need to be shaded in.

The Ferris wheel could make 2 full turns in 12 minutes, 5 full turns in 30 minutes and 7 full turns in 42 minutes.

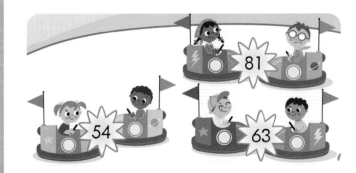

20-21 7, 11 and 12 times tables

It takes 7 days to reach planet 1.
It takes 14 days to reach planet 2.
It takes 21 days to reach planet 3.

The blue rocket needs 55 screws, and the orange rocket needs 33 screws.

Going around the sun:
Jenks takes 108 days to go around 9 times.
Grum takes 56 days to go around 8 times.
Klip takes 35 days to go around 7 times.
Ensk takes 66 days to around 6 times.

The purple team has 84 points
and the blue team has 48 points.

22-23 Number grids

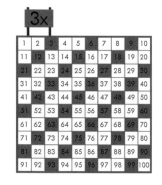
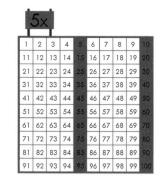

24-25 More practice

There are 24 pea seeds, 50 tomato seeds, and 18 pumpkin seeds.

There are 15 gnomes in stock.

9 tubs will feed 36 plants.

The vine has 8 leaves in total.

3 baskets will hold 12 plants, 9 baskets will hold 36 plants and 12 baskets will hold 48 plants.

From left to right, the plants will eat:
9 flies, 18 flies and 12 flies.

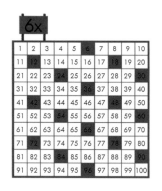

26–27 Quick quizzes

54 seeds	20 fish
35 spots	30 coins
32 petals	6 seagulls
21 stars	90 jewels
	16 crabs

The first array has 20 blocks.
The second array has 21 blocks.
The third array has 48 blocks.
The fourth array has 45 blocks.

$2 \times 5 = 10$	$9 \times 2 = 18$
$6 \times 9 = 54$	$7 \times 8 = 56$
$12 \times 4 = 48$	$10 \times 10 = 100$
$7 \times 3 = 21$	$3 \times 6 = 18$
$8 \times 6 = 48$	

28–29 Sharing it out

Each pirate will get:
3 diamonds, 6 rubies, 1 emerald, 5 rings.

Each cannon can fire 2 times.
2 cannonballs will be left over.

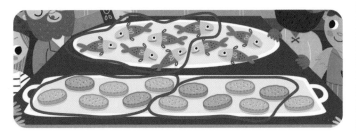

Each pirate will get 1 fish and 2 sea biscuits. There will be 3 fish and 1 sea biscuit left over.

30–31 Take it away

It will take the bear 4 mouthfuls to eat all the fish.

Each marmot will get 6 leaves.

Each pony can carry 3 bags.

Each goat will eat 6 berries.

32–33 Making things smaller

A portion of 10 spiders will cost 10 pennies.

From left to right, the monsters will get 4 cans, 2 cans and 10 cans.

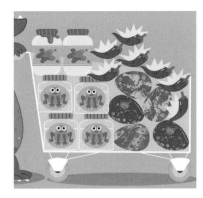

Each monster will get:
2 slime rolls
5 jellied worms
6 earwax crisps
3 toenail bites
1 mud shake.

34–35 Using a number line

The ants can carry 4 leaves between them.

After 5 days, the parrot will have eaten all of the berries.

Each frog will get 5 flies.

36–37 More practice

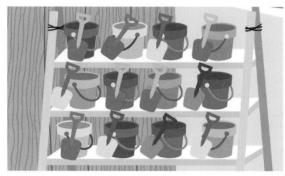

$$12 \div 3 = 4$$

The number missing from the beach balls is 3.

Each person gets 7 shells.

38–39 Quick quizzes

The recipe needs 5 toenail flakes, 7 rotten eggs, 2 jars of mud, 10 slime rolls, and 9 flaming peppers.

3 times, 7 times, 6 times

4 flies, 2 flies

$30 \div 5 = 6$	$100 \div 10 = 10$
$24 \div 8 = 4$	$20 \div 2 = 10$
$63 \div 7 = 9$	$36 \div 6 = 6$
$144 \div 12 = 12$	$40 \div 8 = 5$
$12 \div 4 = 3$	$18 \div 3 = 6$
$90 \div 9 = 10$	$8 \div 4 = 2$
$48 \div 12 = 4$	$99 \div 9 = 11$
$55 \div 11 = 5$	$96 \div 12 = 8$

40–41 Splitting the remainder

Each person gets $\frac{1}{4}$ of the pizza.

Each bowl gets:

$1\frac{1}{4}$ pears, $2\frac{1}{4}$ oranges, $3\frac{3}{4}$ plums

42–43 More practice

4 fairy costumes can be completed, with 1 wing left over.

4 coats can be completed, with 3 buttons left over.

Each hat gets 3 bells, with 2 left over.

4 dinosaur costumes can be completed, with 3 spikes left over.

Each wand gets 3 whole bags of sequins, and the last bag is split into thirds – so each wand gets $3\frac{1}{3}$ bags in total.

44–45 Quick quizzes

$19 \div 2 = 9 \text{ r } 1$ $\qquad$ $27 \div 5 = 5 \text{ r } 2$

$23 \div 3 = 7 \text{ r } 2$ $\qquad$ $58 \div 7 = 8 \text{ r } 2$

$63 \div 10 = 6 \text{ r } 3$ $\qquad$ $33 \div 10 = 3 \text{ r } 3$

$51 \div 4 = 12 \text{ r } 3$ $\qquad$ $29 \div 6 = 4 \text{ r } 5$

$\dfrac{1}{5}$ $\qquad$ $\dfrac{2}{3}$ $\qquad$ $\dfrac{1}{2}$ $\qquad$ $\dfrac{3}{4}$

There will be 1 coin, 4 shells, 2 worms and 5 sweets left over.

$11\dfrac{1}{2}$ $\quad$ $12\dfrac{1}{3}$ $\quad$ $4\dfrac{3}{4}$ $\quad$ $6\dfrac{1}{2}$ $\quad$ $7\dfrac{2}{3}$ $\quad$ $8\dfrac{3}{4}$

46–47 Back and forth

The missing numbers in the pyramids from top to bottom are 7, 12 and 9.

$15 \div 3 = 5$

$5 \times 3 = 15$

$16 \div 4 = 4$

$4 \times 4 = 16$

$24 \div 6 = 4$

$4 \times 6 = 24$

🦎 = 7

△ = 5

$55 \div 11$	$42 \div 7$	$18 \div 3$
$= 5$	$= 6$	$= 6$
11×4	8×7	6×3
$= 44$	$= 56$	$= 18$

This bridge is safe to cross. - - - ->

48–49 More practice

The party game has 9 prizes.

Each party bag will get:
4 stickers
2 candies
1 bouncy ball.

50–51 Bigger numbers

28×2

20 2 8 2

40 16

56

42×3

40 3 2 3

120 6

126

125 bolts and
141 cogs will
be needed.

54-55 More practice

From left to right there are 12, 28 and 36 windows on the towers.

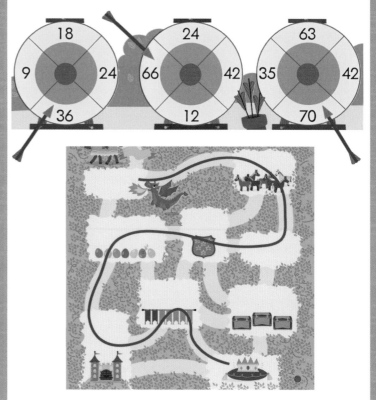

52-53 Quick quizzes

$15 \div 3 = 5$ $8 \times 5 = 40$

$40 \div 5 = 8$ $5 \times 3 = 15$

$70 \div 7 = 10$ $9 \times 4 = 36$

$96 \div 12 = 8$ $5 \times 12 = 60$

$60 \div 5 = 12$ $6 \times 7 = 42$

$42 \div 6 = 7$ $12 \times 8 = 96$

$36 \div 9 = 4$ $10 \times 7 = 70$

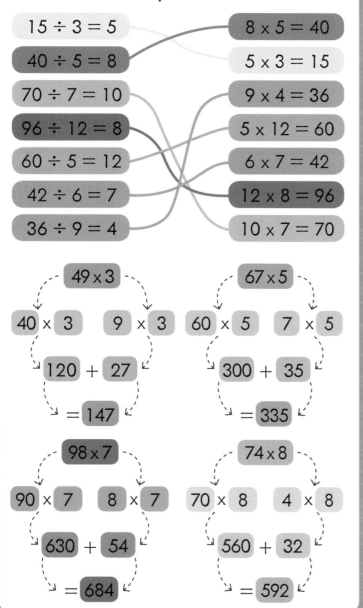

49×3

40×3 9×3

$120 + 27$

$= 147$

67×5

60×5 7×5

$300 + 35$

$= 335$

98×7

90×7 8×7

$630 + 54$

$= 684$

74×8

70×8 4×8

$560 + 32$

$= 592$

56-57 More practice

Edited by Rosie Dickins   Managing designer: Zoe Wray

First published in 2019 by Usborne Publishing Ltd., 83-85 Saffron Hill, London, EC1N 8RT, England. www.usborne.com Copyright © 2019 Usborne Publishing Ltd.

Make it bigger

Add the right number of flasks of motor oil to the trays to power the robots on page 6.

More practice

Add these cookies to the baking tray to create an array on page 8.

More practice

Add two bows to each of the dogs on page 12.

Times tables 2, 4, 8

Add two snails to each of the leaves on page 14.

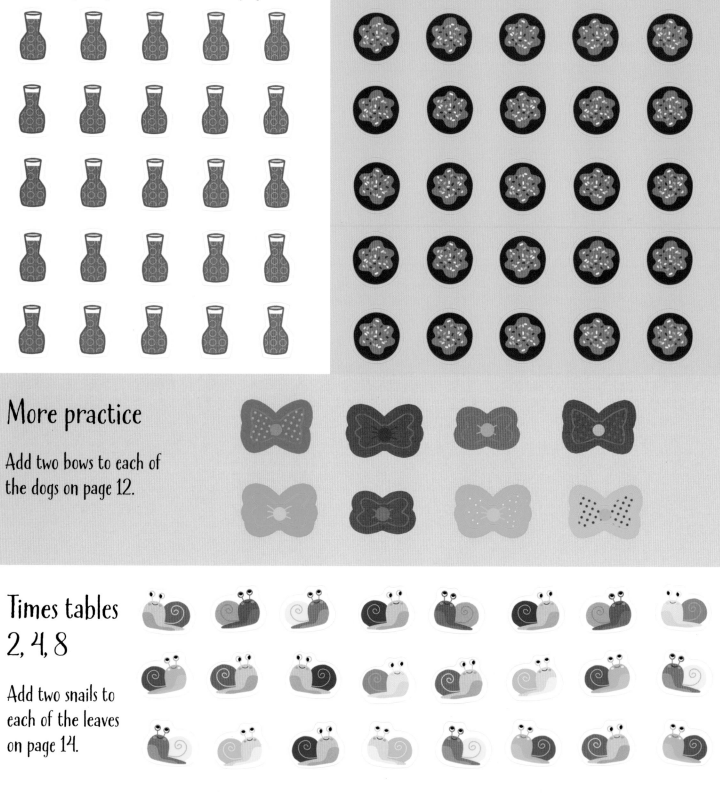

Times tables 2, 4, 8

Add enough flies for the spiders to each web on page 15.

Times tables 3, 6, 9

Add these stickers to the coconuts in the 3x table on page 18.

Add these crashes to the right bumper cars on page 19.

54　81　63

Take it away

Add panels to the rocket ships on page 20.

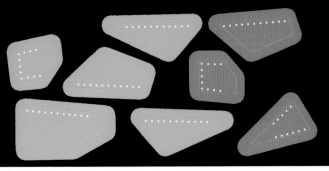

More practice

Add 3 more sets of leaves to the plant on page 13.

Making things smaller

Add the right number of ingredients to the monster's shopping trolley on page 33.

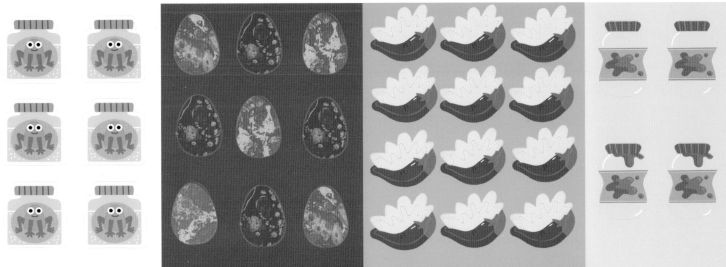

Using a number line

Add enough leaves so that there are 3 ants per leaf on page 34.

More practice

Add these bucket and spade sets so that each shelf has the same number, on page 36.

More practice

Add these wings to the fairy costumes on page 42.

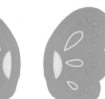

More practice

Share out the chocolate stars equally between the cupcakes on page 48.

More practice

Give the ribbon to the winner of pin the tail on the donkey on page 49.

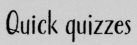

Bigger numbers

Add these cogs to the machines on page 50.

(2) (8) (3)

(16) (56)

(40) (120) (6)

Quick quizzes

Add a star sticker to the 'Quick quizzes' pages each time you complete a quiz. Use extras wherever you like.

More practice

Add arrows to the biggest number on the targets on page 54.